"The AI Bible, make money with artificial intelligence:

Real case studies and instructions for implementation. "

imprint

Editor:

John du Jardin

SDCJAK CO., LTD

3/7 Sukhumvit Soi 18, 10110 Bangkok, Thailand

info@thaipan-legal.com

Foreword

In today's world, Artificial Intelligence (AI) offers a plethora of opportunities for individuals and individuals to increase their income and grow their wealth. From the use of AI-based trading tools and investment advisory services to the automated creation of text and images through intelligent technologies, the application of AI has the potential to revolutionize the way we make money and manage our finances.

This book is intended to give you an overview of how you as a private individual can benefit from the various options. We won't just limit ourselves to the world of finance, but also explore other areas where AI-based technologies can be used to increase earning potential.

In this book, I will introduce different methods and tools based on AI to help you increase your income. I will show you how to use AI-based text generation tools and image generation tools to produce high-quality content and graphics for your online presence.

Furthermore, we will talk about how you can use AI-based translation services to translate texts into different languages quickly and effectively, and how you can use AI-based chatbots and automation tools.

The work aims to give you a comprehensive overview of how you can use AI-based technologies to increase your income and spice up your finances. I will introduce you to different tools and methods you can use to increase your productivity and better serve your customers. Overall, this book offers practical guidance for individuals and private individuals who want to make money with AI, automated if possible. It will help you understand the different possibilities that AI-based technologies offer.

Let's talk numbers! Attached are some screenshots of my personal earnings, 100% generated by AI tools and the application of artificial intelligence.

eBook-Tantiemen	Tantiemen für Druckausgaben	KENP-Tantiemen	Tantiemen Insgesamt	Tantiemen insgesamt - EUR
€1,346.73	€7,597.25	€9.50	€8,953.48	€8,953.48

There are numerous ways to make money with AI. Whether it's content creation, image generation or application development, the possibilities are only limited by your creativity. And the best part is that most of the revenue is generated passively.

It is important to me to tell you about my failures and failures. Because it was from these experiences that I learned the most and was able to expand my knowledge.

My goal is to inspire, motivate and support you. I want to help you achieve your goals and be successful.

In this book, I'm going to detail the 3 ways I've used to make mostly passive income with AI.

Introduction

You've taken an important step in learning more about this technology and understanding how you can use it to make money online.

In this book, you'll learn everything you need to know to take advantage of AI's opportunities and differentiate yourself from the competition. Whether you just want to earn a few hundred euros part-time or want to build a sustainable online business, you will learn strategies for all scenarios and be able to decide for yourself which path is right for you.

Whether you're a complete beginner who's never started an online project or you're looking to increase your income from existing projects, this book will teach you everything you need to be successful.

First, you will learn the basic concepts of AI and learn more about the opportunities and challenges it brings. You will understand how AI works and the impact it is having on the way we work and make money today.

At the heart of the book, you will be introduced to lucrative methods with which you can earn money through the use of AI. You will also learn some Power AI tools that will help you to optimize your work and make it more effective.

But not only the methods and strategies are important. I will also show you how to optimize your mindset to establish a successful business model. You will learn how to best use your time and energy, and how to best use your skills and talents.

Are you ready to use the possibilities of AI and earn money online? Then this book is for you! Let's get started!

1.1 What is AI?

Artificial Intelligence (AI) is a field of computer science that deals with the development of intelligent machines and software. The goal of AI is to program machines and computers to be able to simulate human-like behavior and thinking.

AI systems are developed using algorithms and technologies such as machine learning, neural networks and natural language processing. These systems can analyze data and information and make decisions and carry out actions on this basis.

There are different types of AI systems, including weak AI, strong AI, and cognitive systems.

Weak AI is specific to a specific task or problem and operates within these narrowly defined boundaries. An example of weak AI is speech recognition. In this case, the AI specializes in recognizing speech and converting it into text or speech.

Strong AI, on the other hand, can solve complex problems and simulate human-like thinking and behavior. Strong AI systems can learn and make decisions independently. There is currently no strong AI on the market.

Cognitive systems are a type of AI that can integrate human knowledge and understanding into the systems. These systems can understand, learn and apply human knowledge. Cognitive systems can be used in medicine, for example, to help doctors diagnose and treat diseases.

AI is now used in many fields, including medicine, automotive, financial services, image and speech recognition, and robotics and automation.

In medicine, for example, AI can be used to improve the diagnosis and treatment of diseases. AI systems can analyze patient data and help doctors make the right decisions.

In the automotive industry, AI can be used to develop autonomous vehicles. These vehicles can navigate independently and make decisions to avoid accidents.

In the financial services industry, AI can be used to mitigate risk and improve the efficiency of processes. For example, AI systems can be used to assess credit risk or make trading decisions.

Image and speech recognition are other important areas of application for AI. These technologies can be used, for example, in security monitoring or in the automatic translation of texts.

Robotics and automation are also important application areas of AI. AI systems can be used in factory automation, for example, to automate processes and increase productivity.

Source: https://pixabay.com

1.2 Fields of application of AI today

Artificial intelligence (AI) can be found in many areas and industries today and is being used in more and more fields of application. Here are some of the most important fields of application of AI today:

Healthcare: AI is being used in healthcare to improve the diagnosis and treatment of diseases. For example, AI-based diagnostic systems can help identify diseases earlier and recommend better treatment options. AI can also be used in medical research to develop new therapies and medicines.

Automotive industry: AI is used in the automotive industry to develop autonomous vehicles. For example, AI systems can navigate independently and make decisions to avoid accidents. AI can also be used in the production of vehicles to optimize processes and increase efficiency.

Financial Services: AI is used in the financial services industry to mitigate risk and improve the efficiency of processes. For example, AI systems can be used to assess credit risk or make trading decisions. AI is also used in the financial sector to combat fraud and analyze customers.

Image and speech recognition: AI is also used in image and speech recognition. These technologies can be used, for example, in security monitoring or in the automatic translation of texts. Image recognition can also be used to detect diseases in medical images or to analyze products in industry.

Marketing and advertising: AI is used in marketing and advertising to create personalized campaigns and analyze customer behavior. For example, AI systems can analyze customer behavior patterns and create personalized offers.

Retail: AI is used in retail to analyze customer needs and create personalized offers. AI-based systems can, for example, make recommendations for products or carry out price optimization.

Robotics and Automation: AI is also used in robotics and automation. AI systems can be used in factory automation, for example, to automate processes and increase productivity. AI-based systems are also used in logistics and transport to optimize processes.

The areas of application of AI are diverse and are playing an increasingly important role in many industries. From medicine to the automotive industry to retail and the financial sector, there are numerous fields of application for AI.

1.3 The societal dimension of AI: A critical examination

The future of AI is undoubtedly full of opportunities and challenges that will impact our daily lives on an unprecedented scale. We are at the beginning of a new era in which groundbreaking technologies and innovations will shape our lives. It is crucial that we are clear about the possibilities and challenges of AI to shape a future that is beneficial for all of us.

The fields of application of AI are diverse and range from healthcare and transport to business and education. AI will change the way we live, work and interact, helping us increase efficiency, provide personalized solutions and solve problems. But despite all the euphoria about the potential of AI, we must not lose sight of the challenges and risks.

When we talk about artificial intelligence, there are also some dangers and challenges that we should talk about. An example of a hazard could be machines making decisions that are not fair or discriminatory. There is a risk that AI systems will make discriminatory decisions based on unconscious biases and inequalities in the training data. Strict ethical standards and regulations are necessary here to ensure that AI systems act fairly and equitably.

Another danger could be that machines know us better through our behavior than we know ourselves. AI systems can predict our behavior and preferences based on data analysis and pattern recognition. This could lead to a restriction of our freedom and privacy. Here, transparent and responsible data use and storage is necessary to protect our privacy.

Another example of a challenge with AI is that while the machines are excellent at recognizing patterns and making predictions, they cannot always understand the context. This can lead to wrong decisions that are dangerous or unethical. It is therefore important to feed the AI systems with enough context and background knowledge so that they can make informed decisions.

These are just a few examples of AI challenges and risks, but there are many more we need to consider. We must be aware of these challenges and dangers to ensure a future-proof and ethical use of AI. We must responsibly and carefully drive the development of AI systems and technologies to create a safe and sustainable future for all of us. But despite these challenges, the future of AI is undoubtedly bright. In medicine, for example, AI systems can help diagnose diseases by evaluating medical images and data. AI systems can also be used to support patient therapy by creating personalized therapy plans.

There is also a lot of potential for AI in the mobility sector. Self-driving cars can improve road safety by being able to react to traffic situations faster and more precisely than human drivers. In addition, they can make traffic flow more smoothly and thus contribute to less congestion and traffic congestion.

In business, AI can contribute to increasing efficiency by automating and optimizing processes. By analyzing large amounts of data, companies can also develop personalized solutions for their customers and thus increase customer satisfaction.

There is also a lot of potential for AI in the field of education. For example, it can help with the personalization of learning content and thus take individual strengths and weaknesses into account. In addition, AI systems can help with the evaluation of assignments and tests, thus saving teachers and lecturers time.

However, we must realize that AI is not the solution to all problems. Human decisions are still needed to evaluate and validate the results of AI systems. We also need to ensure that AI is used ethically and responsibly.

Overall, AI will profoundly change the way we live, work and interact. It is our responsibility as a society to ensure that these changes are made for of all.

1.4 What the AI cannot do?

Despite the many advances in AI technology, there are still many things that AI cannot do. One of the greatest challenges of AI is to understand and replicate the human mind and intuition. Here are some of the things the AI can't do:

Emotional intelligence: The AI is unable to feel or understand emotions such as love, hate, joy, sadness, and jealousy. Although there are already some AI systems that attempt to recognize human emotions, they fail to capture the subtle nuances and complexities of human emotions.

Creativity: Creativity is a human ability that is difficult to define and reproduce. Although there are already some AI systems capable of generating artworks or music, these works are often not as original and unique as human art.

Moral Judgment: The AI is incapable of making moral judgments. Although there are already some AI systems that try to make moral decisions, their decisions are based on predefined rules and algorithms programmed by humans. As such, they are often unable to resolve complex moral dilemmas that require human judgment.

Physical Sensations: The AI is unable to feel physical sensations such as pain, hunger, or thirst. Although there are already some AI systems capable of emulating human senses such as sight, hearing and smell, they cannot grasp the complexity and subtlety of human sensations.

Human Interaction: The AI can not completely replace human interaction. Although there are already some AI systems capable of understanding and communicating human speech, they cannot fully capture and replace human experience.

Self-Reflection: The AI is unable to self-reflect and improve. Although there are already some AI systems capable of improving their own decisions and algorithms, they lack the human capacity for self-reflection and the ability to self-improve.

However, these limitations do not mean that AI is not useful or even necessary. AI can help us solve complex problems, make decisions and increase our efficiency. However, it is important to be aware that AI cannot do everything and that it still needs to be controlled by human hands. Another area where AI is still limited is in empathy. Although there have been some advances in the development of systems that can recognize emotions and moods, the ability to feel and show empathy is still an ability unique to humans. People may be able to interpret subtle emotional cues, such as body language and tone of voice, and show empathic responses based on those cues. Machines, on the other hand, can recognize and respond to emotions, but they are unable to create a true emotional connection with a human individual.

In addition, there are also cases in which AI systems can produce incorrect or unforeseen results. An example of this is the so-called "bias" problem. If the data sets on which the AI is trained contain certain biases or discriminations, this can result in the system adopting and reproducing those biases. A famous example of this is the case of Amazon, which had developed an AI-powered job evaluation tool that discriminated against women because it was trained on datasets authored primarily by men.

Another limitation of AI is creativity. Although AI systems are capable of recognizing patterns and making predictions, they still lack real creative ability. They cannot create original ideas or concepts that are not in their datasets. Creativity requires a kind of human consciousness that is currently unattainable for AI systems.

Finally, there are also some practical limitations with AI due to their limited hardware and power supplies. AI systems require a lot of computing power and storage space to perform their tasks, which often can be expensive and energy-intensive. This can result in AI systems being impractical or uneconomical for certain applications.

In summary, while AI has tremendous potential in many areas, it also has its limitations and limitations. There are many things that AI systems cannot do, including creative tasks, empathy, and ethical decision-making. It is important to be aware of and consider these limitations when designing and deploying AI systems to ensure that they are not only effective but responsible.

2. Earn money with ChatGPT

When it comes to using AI as a freelancer, it can seem intimidating and complicated at first. But don't worry, there is an easy way to make serious money with AI without requiring large seed capital or coding skills.

Firstly, you should understand what AI is and how it works. AI, or artificial intelligence, refers to machines and algorithms capable of performing human-like tasks. AI systems can collect, analyze and use data to make decisions and solve problems.

As a freelancer, you can use AI to optimize your work process and make it more efficient. An example of this is the automation of recurring tasks, such as creating invoices or composing emails. By delegating these tasks to AI systems, you can save time and focus on your core competencies.

Another benefit of AI is the ability to analyze data and trends to make better decisions. For example, if you work as a social media manager, you can use AI systems to collect and analyze data about your audience's engagement and interactions. Based on this information, you can then make strategic decisions to optimize your social media presence and attract more customers.

Now for the simple method of earning serious money with AI: You can register as a freelancer on platforms like Upwork or Freelancer.com and offer your services. Here, you can search specifically for jobs that are AI-related, such as the development of chatbots or the creation of machine learning models.

You don't have to be a proven expert to be successful in this field. It is sufficient if you have basic knowledge of the relevant technologies and are willing to continue your education and learn.

In summary, AI offers tremendous potential for freelancers to work more effectively and productively while making more money. If you specialize in AI-related projects as a freelancer and continue to educate yourself, you can be successful in this area and earn a stable income.

2.1. What you should know before you jump into the program

ChatGPT is a very advanced chatbot based on artificial intelligence. However, there are still many mistakes that can be made when dealing with ChatGPT. The following article will discuss some of these errors and how to avoid them.

Misunderstandings due to wrong input

One of the most common sources of error when dealing with ChatGPT is entering incorrect information. If you are not careful and formulate your questions or answers unclearly, misunderstandings can arise. While ChatGPT is capable of understanding natural language, it is not perfect and cannot always correctly interpret the context. To avoid misunderstandings, you should formulate your questions and answers clearly and precisely.

Wrong expectations

Another common mistake is having wrong expectations of ChatGPT. ChatGPT is a computer program that has its limitations. He cannot answer all questions and cannot solve all problems. One should have realistic expectations of ChatGPT and not expect it to act like a human interlocutor.

Lack of courtesy

Although ChatGPT is just a computer program, it's important to treat it politely. One should treat him the same as a human interlocutor and not be rude or disrespectful. It's important to remember that ChatGPT is also just a tool, and its job is to answer questions and solve problems.

data protection

Another important factor when dealing with ChatGPT is privacy. ChatGPT may contain sensitive data such as names, addresses, or credit card information. It is important to ensure that this data is safe and secure. One should only use ChatGPT on secure networks and make sure that it does not reveal any personal information.

Overreliance on ChatGPT

Another mistake is to rely too much on ChatGPT. ChatGPT is a useful tool, but it's important to take advantage of other resources as well. It is important to do your research and consult other sources as well. One should consider ChatGPT as part of the bigger picture and not as the only source of information.

In summary, it is important to be aware of the mistakes that can be made when dealing with ChatGPT. One should ensure that one treats ChatGPT courteously, has realistic expectations, asks clear and concise questions, complies with privacy regulations, and is not overly dependent on him. By avoiding these errors, one can use the full potential of ChatGPT and have a positive experience.

2.2 How does ChatGPT work

ChatGPT is an advanced Artificial Intelligence (AI) specialized in having human-like conversations with users. This AI technology makes it possible to understand, analyze and respond to human speech. In this article, we will take a look at how ChatGPT works.

The technology behind ChatGPT is called Deep Learning. This is a sub-area of machine learning based on neural networks. ChatGPT uses a special transformer network that is optimized for processing texts. It is designed so that it can be trained to use natural language, thus being able to hold human-like conversations.

To train ChatGPT, it needs a large amount of training data. This data can come from various sources, such as publicly available texts or chat histories. The network analyzes the data and thereby learns the patterns and connections between the words and sentences.

Now, when a user asks a question to the chatbot, this question will be analyzed by ChatGPT. The AI looks for the training data and uses the knowledge it has learned to generate a suitable answer. The context in which the question was asked is also considered.

The Transformer network is designed to learn continuously. This means that the chatbot evolves and improves with every conversation it has. This makes it possible to give more and more accurate and appropriate answers.

To ensure ChatGPT works effectively and securely, training data must be carefully selected and monitored. If the data is insufficient or unrepresentative, the chatbot cannot work effectively. It is also important to take proper security precautions to protect the chatbot and users' data.

Overall, ChatGPT offers an effective and user-friendly way to interact with users. With its ability to have human-like conversations, it's a powerful tool for businesses looking to improve their customer interactions. As technology continues to evolve, ChatGPT will become even more powerful and versatile in the future.

2.3 Write non-fiction books with ChatGPT and sell them on Amazon

Using artificial intelligence (AI) like ChatGPT can be a valuable resource for writers and readers. ChatGPT can help to quickly find information, generate ideas and even write text. However, there are also some mistakes that should be avoided when using ChatGPT when dealing with books.

Firstly, we should be aware that the AI is not yet perfect, and its capabilities are limited. There are many factors that can affect the quality of the AI-generated texts, such as: B. the quality of the underlying data, the type of text and the input parameters. It is therefore unlikely that an AI like ChatGPT can write a complete book that meets the high demands of the readers and the market.

Another mistake in using ChatGPT is that some authors try to use the AI as a substitute for their skills and knowledge. If an author simply inputs an idea and then expects ChatGPT to write the entire book without having to contribute anything themselves, the result will most likely be disappointing. It will always take a pinch of human influence to put the finishing touches to the text. An AI like ChatGPT can serve as a tool to support and enhance the author, but it should not be used as a substitute for human creativity and knowledge.

Another mistake is that some authors use ChatGPT purely as a research source and then simply copy and paste the text without then proofreading it. It is important that authors are aware that ChatGPT is not a license for the unthinking adoption of texts from the Internet.

However, there are exceptions to the rule that ChatGPT should not be used for full book creation. Especially for reference books or technical manuals, ChatGPT can be one of the most valuable resources developed in this decade. In these cases, ChatGPT can be used as a basis for an initial rough draft of the text, which the author can then revise and expand upon to ensure the text is complete and accurate.

In summary, ChatGPT and other AI technologies, if used properly, can be used to produce tons of books in a short amount of time. It is important to be aware that AI is not yet perfect and that it should be used as a tool to support and augment human capabilities. Authors should strive to strengthen their skills and knowledge and use AI as a complement to take the quality of their work to the next level.

2.4. What is a non-fiction book anyway?

A non-fiction book is a book that deals with a specific topic or question and conveys information in the process. Unlike fiction, non-fiction is about conveying knowledge and facts. Non-fiction books can be published on many subject areas, such as history, science, technology, philosophy, psychology, or even health.

Non-fiction books are often structured in terms of content and may also contain charts, tables, graphics, or photos to better illustrate the information. The aim of a non-fiction book is to give the reader a more profound understanding of the subject. A non-fiction book can also contain personal experiences and opinions of the author, but these are always based on facts and scientific knowledge.

2.5 Then let's write

Here is a simple example of how you can use ChatGPT to create texts:

Let's say you're a blogger and you want to write an article about the benefits of yoga. You already have some ideas in your head, but you don't know exactly how to put them into words. This is where ChatGPT can help you!

Open a chat platform or website where you can interact with ChatGPT. There are different ways to use ChatGPT, such as via OpenAI, Hugging Face or other platforms. Alternatively click here!

Formulate your request to ChatGPT. In this case, you could ask ChatGPT, "Can you tell me some benefits of yoga?" Or, "Could you help me write an article about the health benefits of yoga?"

ChatGPT will now try to understand your request and give you an answer. ChatGPT may give you multiple answers to choose from.

Read ChatGPT's response and edit if necessary. While ChatGPT can help you structure your thoughts and put your ideas into words, it's important that you check the text for accuracy and make adjustments if necessary.

Use ChatGPT as a tool to strengthen your writing. ChatGPT can help you improve your writing style and refine your ideas.

Save the text you created with ChatGPT and continue editing later. You can use the text as a basis for your article and further adapt and improve it if necessary.

ChatGPT can be a useful support for structuring ideas and writing texts. However, one should keep in mind that ChatGPT is not a substitute for writing your own and human verification is still necessary to ensure the accuracy and quality of the text.

Incidentally, it was not I who wrote the last paragraph, but ChatGPT. cool right?

2.6 How are the texts created? And what the hell are prompts?

Prompts are an essential component of using ChatGPT, a machine learning system specialized in natural language generation. Thanks to prompts, ChatGPT can be specifically trained to generate texts that are tailored to specific requirements and contexts.

Prompts are text inputs that the model uses as a starting point for generating text. These can be simple questions, complex inquiries, or even longer texts. The model uses the information from the prompt to generate an appropriate answer or text. The model is based on the structure and context of the prompt to generate the most meaningful and logical answer possible.

Prompts can be used in a variety of ways to train ChatGPT for specific needs. For example, a simple prompt might be a simple question like "What is the name of the highest mountain in the world?" The model uses the prompt to generate a short and precise answer, such as "The highest mountain in the world is Mount Everest."

A more complex prompt can be longer text, such as a product description for an online store. The model uses the prompt to generate a description that embeds the product in the context of the shop and the target group. The model considers the language and spelling of the shop, as well as the specific features and benefits of the product.

Prompts can also be used for creative writing projects. For example, an author can use a prompt to ask ChatGPT to generate a new character description for a story. The model then uses the information from the prompt to create a character that fits the story and its contexts.

Another benefit of prompts is that they allow the model to be tailored to specific audiences. For example, a company can use ChatGPT to generate marketing texts for different customer groups. The model uses different prompts to generate texts that are tailored to the respective target groups.

However, there are also some challenges when using prompts. Thus, the prompts must be concise and well-structured to generate a meaningful and targeted response. Furthermore, the model can sometimes have trouble handling complex or unclear prompts, which can lead to undesirable results.

Prompts are a powerful way to tailor ChatGPT to specific needs and contexts. With concise and well-structured prompts, users can leverage the model to generate high-quality, well-targeted text suitable for a variety of applications.

2.7 A list of essential prompts for long format texts

1. "I need a [type of blog post] that provides my [ideal customer persona] with valuable and relevant information and convinces them to take [desired action] on my [website/product]."
2. "I'm looking for a [blog post type] that will engage my [ideal customer persona] with a unique and compelling perspective on [topic] and convince them to take [desired actions] on my [website/product]. seize."
3. "I'm looking for a [blog post type] that will enlighten my [ideal customer persona] on a certain [topic] and convince them to take [desired action] on my [website/product]."
4. "I need a [type of blog post] that directly addresses my [ideal customer persona]'s needs and pain points and convinces them to take [desired action] with a sense of urgency and a strong proposition."
5. "I'm looking for a [type of blog post] that presents [ideal customer personas] with the value and benefits of my [product/service] and convinces them to take [desired action] with social proof and credibility. components."
6. "I need a [type of blog post] that tells a story about my [product/service] and how it helped [the ideal customer persona] achieve their [goal] in an understandable and engaging way."
7. "I need a [type of blog post] that tells a story about my [product/service] and how it helped [the ideal customer persona] achieve their [goal] in a relatable and engaging way."
8. "I'm looking for a [blog post type] that attracts my [ideal customer persona] with a strong headline and hook, and then convinces them to take [desired action] with compelling language and compelling evidence."
9. "I need a [blog post type] that addresses my [ideal customer persona]'s pain points and needs and shows them that my [product/service] is the solution they were looking for."
10. "I'm looking for a [blog post type] that clearly explains [the ideal customer persona]'s features and benefits of my [product/service] and

provides them with a strong call-to-action."

11. "I need a [type of blog post] that will overcome objections and concerns my [ideal customer persona] may have about my [product/service] and convince them to take [desired action]."

12. "I'm looking for a [type of blog post] that will showcase [ideal customer persona] the unique features and benefits of my [product/service] and convince them to make a purchase."

13. "I need a [type of blog post] that arouses my [ideal customer persona] [emotions] about my [product/service] and convinces them to take [desired action] with a sense of urgency."

14. "I'm looking for a [blog post type] that builds trust and credibility with my [ideal customer persona] by highlighting the successes and testimonials of previous customers who have used my [product/service]."

15. "I need a [type of blog post] that will convince my [ideal customer persona] to buy my [product/service] by highlighting its unique benefits and addressing any potential objections."

16. "I'm looking for a [blog post type] that speaks directly to my [ideal customer persona] and convinces them to take [desired action] on my [website/product]."

2.8 Step-By-Step Guide

1. Decide on a topic/niche

I won't go into too much detail on niche research as it isn't part of the actual ChatGPT application. Nevertheless, here is a small introduction. You will also find sufficient information on the topic in the chapter section on keyword research. You need niche research to find a topic for your non-fiction book that you can sell successfully and as competitively as possible on Amazon KDP and around the world.

Amazon KDP (Kindle Direct Publishing) is an Amazon self-publishing service that allows authors and publishers to sell their books as eBooks or print-on-demand books directly to readers around the world.

With KDP, authors can upload their book, design the cover and determine the price themselves. They can also choose whether they want to sell their book exclusively through Amazon or also make it available on other platforms such as Apple iBooks or Barnes & Noble Nook.

KDP offers a variety of tools and resources to help authors get their books published, including the ability to run marketing promotions like free promotion days and countdown deals, and run ad campaigns through Amazon Advertising.

KDP gives authors the ability to bring their books to a global audience without the need for a publishing deal. It's a great way for new and independent writers to make their voices heard and share their stories with the world.

To find a profitable niche for Kindle Direct Publishing (KDP), thorough keyword research is key. The goal is to find keywords that have sufficient search volume, but at the same time are not too competitive.

The first step is choosing the main subject or genre for your book. For example, if you wanted to write a non-fiction book about healthy eating, the main topic would be "health" or "nutrition."

Next, using keyword tools like Mangools KWFinder, you should work out which keywords are relevant to your main topic and how often they are searched for. It is important to find keywords with a sufficiently high search volume. Ideally, these keywords have at least 500+ monthly searches.

It's also important to pay attention to keyword ranking to determine the level of competition. If many other books are already ranking for that keyword, then it will be harder for your book to appear on the first page of search results.

This is where it helps to analyze the competition at the top positions and focus on finding less competitive keywords that don't already have a strong bid. It's about finding a niche in which you can establish yourself as a writer.

To find the right combination of keywords, you should also use Google's autocomplete function. Just type the main keyword into Google's search box and see what auto-suggestions come up. These suggestions will show you which keywords other users are searching for often and can be a valuable source of niche ideas.

In summary, keyword research is an important step in finding a profitable KDP niche. By finding keywords with a sufficiently high search volume and low competition intensity, you can establish yourself as an author in your niche and successfully place your book on the market.

3. The best tool for keyword research - the KWFinder by Mangools

QR-Code KWFINDER

KWFinder is a powerful keyword research tool developed by Mangools. It's easy to use and packed with features that make it one of the best tools out there.

Why KWFinder is the best keyword research tool in my experience:

user-friendliness

KWFinder is easy to use and has a user-friendly interface. Even if you are not an SEO expert, you will easily understand how the tool works and how you can use it to find the right keywords for your project.

accuracy

KWFinder provides accurate data on search volume, CPC (cost-per-click) and competition. This information is critical to choosing the right keywords for your campaign and ensuring you're getting the most of your marketing budget.

Keyword and trend analysis

With KWFinder you can analyze your keywords and identify trends. You can also find out which keywords are being used by your competitors and how searches have changed over time. This information is critical to developing an effective keyword strategy.

Local Searches

If you have a local business, you can use KWFinder to search for keywords specific to your area. This will help you better reach your target audience and increase your chances of a higher conversion rate.

Budget-friendly

Compared to other keyword research tools, KWFinder is very attractively priced and also offers a free trial.

By the way, you can get the tool here: https://mangools.com

To find potential niches for your KDP book, there are a few steps you can follow:

Enter the subject of your book in the search box

Enter the subject of your book or a keyword that describes it in the search box. The KWFinder will then return a list of related keywords.

Filter the results by relevance and difficulty

Now, it's important to filter the results to find out which keywords are the most relevant and at the same time the least competitive. You can do this by filtering the results by relevance and difficulty. The keyword with the highest search volume and lowest difficulty is usually the ideal keyword to include in your book description or title.

3. Incorporate the keyword into your book description and title

Once you've found the ideal keyword, you should incorporate it into your book description and title to ensure your target audience finds the publication.

The best free alternative, which, it must be said, does not give the best results, but still provides some data that can be useful, is Google's "Keyword Planner".

3. Write or let ChatGPT write the text!

There are different approaches to writing long format texts.

After a lot of trial and error and hours in front of the computer, I can give you step-by-step instructions on how to do this. My method is certainly not the only one, but it is proven. For a better understanding, let's work directly with an example. We would like to write a book on the subject of "diet with gout".

1st Prompt - "Write an outline for a book about a book on dieting with gout"

Result: I. Introduction

Description of gout and how it is related to diet

Presentation of the book and its purpose

II. What is gout?

Definition of gout and its causes

symptoms and diagnosis

Treatment options and their effectiveness

III. Relationship between diet and gout

Dietary factors that can trigger or worsen gout

Recommended dietary guidelines for people with gout

Important foods and nutrients for a healthy gout diet

IV. Recipes for a gout-friendly diet

breakfast recipes

Lunch and Dinner Recipes

Snack ideas for in between

desserts and drinks

V. Lifestyle changes to prevent and treat gout

Exercises and activities that can relieve gout symptoms

Stress attachment techniques and their impact on gout

Weight management and its importance in preventing gout

VI. Conclusion and outlook

Summary of the main points from the book

Outlook on future developments in the research and treatment of gout

Final recommendations and advice for people with gout and their loved ones

The output for the introduction is impressive. A little tweaking and the text is ready to be copied: Welcome to this book about gout, a painful condition caused by a buildup of uric acid crystals in the joints. In this book, we will take an in-depth look at all aspects of gout, from its causes and symptoms to diagnosis, treatment, and prevention.

In the first few chapters, we'll cover the basics of gout, including a detailed explanation of what gout is and how it develops. We'll also look at the risk factors for gout, including lifestyle and dietary factors, as well as genetic factors. In addition, we will examine the differences between acute and chronic gout and how they affect treatment.

As we continue through the book, we will look at the various symptoms of gout, such as pain, swelling, and redness in the affected joints. We will also discuss the potential complications of gout, such as kidney stones and kidney failure, as well as the impact it has on overall health.

Another important topic is the diagnosis of gout, including the various tests and investigations that can be done to identify gout. We will also examine the different treatment options for gout, such as medication, dietary changes, and lifestyle changes. We will also discuss alternative treatment options and complementary therapies that can be used to support conventional treatment.

Finally, we will look at the prevention of gout, including the steps that can be taken to reduce the risk of gout. We will also discuss the importance of regular check-ups and screening tests for people at risk.

Overall, this book provides a comprehensive and informative resource for anyone dealing with gout or seeking a more profound understanding of the condition. We hope this book will help you recognize the symptoms of gout and understand how to effectively treat and prevent it.

3. Once you or ChatGPT have finished writing your book, all you have to do is publish the work on Amazon. I just want to touch on that briefly here. I recommend you to watch some YouTube videos. You can find detailed instructions for self-publishers on the platform.

To publish a book to Amazon KDP, you can follow the steps below:

Sign up for an Amazon KDP account: Go to the KDP website (https://kdp.amazon.com/) and click "Sign In" or "Create Account" to create a new account.

Create your book: Write your book in a word processor like Microsoft Word or Google Docs. Make sure your book is saved in a common eBook format like .doc, .docx, .epub, or .pdf.

Formatting your book: Format your book so that it's suitable for e-book sale. Amazon offers a free tool called Kindle Create that can help you format your book.

Cover Design: Design a professional cover for your book. You can either create a cover yourself or have it designed by a professional designer.

Upload your book to Amazon KDP: Sign in to your KDP account and click Create New eBook. Then upload your book and cover and fill out the required metadata.

Review your book: Before you publish your book, you should preview the book on Amazon KDP. Check that everything is formatted correctly, and the cover art is displayed correctly.

Publish your book: Click Publish to publish your book on Amazon KDP.

After you publish your book, it usually takes a few hours for it to be available on Amazon. You can then set the price and promote your book to generate sales.

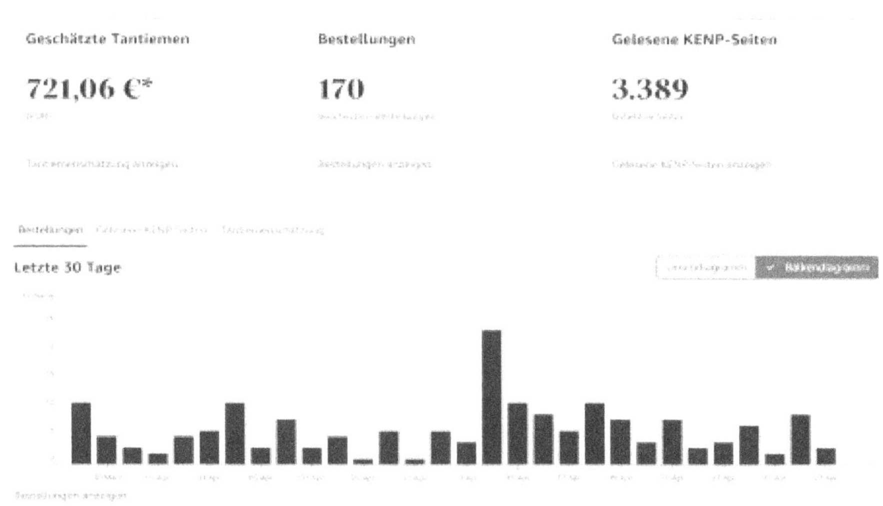

Source: My earnings in April 2023 screenshot

https://kdpreports.amazon.com/dashboard

With the steps listed above, you can already bring your work to the German market. My insider tip at this point? Why not make your expert book accessible worldwide? Very few users deal with publishing outside the reach of the book giant Amazon. But that's where the potential lies. I generate about 40% of my sales outside of Amazon. Best of all, global publishing is even easier than publishing with KDP. The D2D platform takes care of everything. Draft2Digital is a self-publishing platform that helps authors publish their books in various eBook formats. The platform is easy to use and allows authors to sell their books on various online bookstores such as Amazon, Barnes & Noble and Kobo.

To start working with Draft2Digital, authors simply need to create an account and upload their book to the system. The platform then converts the book into various eBook formats and allows authors to customize their book's cover and description.

Once the book is successfully uploaded to the system, authors can list it for sale in various online bookstores. Draft2Digital also offers professional services such as editing, cover design and marketing support. Everything is included in their system and free of charge.

Overall, Draft2Digital is a great option for authors who want to quickly and easily publish their books in various eBook formats. The platform also offers a variety of tools and services to help authors successfully market and sell their book.

Publishing with Draft2Digital is the same as publishing with Amazon KDP. The following steps are necessary:

Create an Account: Go to the Draft2Digital website (https://www.draft2digital.com/book-publishing) and create a free account.

Upload your book: Upload your book file and cover to Draft2Digital. The book should be saved in a common eBook format such as .doc, .docx, .epub, or .pdf.

Formatting the book: Draft2Digital also offers free formatting tools to prepare the book for e-book sale. You can use these or format your book file yourself.

Fill out the metadata: Enter the required information such as book title, author name, description, and categories.

Choose Selling Platforms: You can choose which platforms you want to sell your book on, such as Amazon, Apple Books, Kobo, Barnes & Noble, Tolino, and more.

Check your book: Before publishing, you should preview your book on Draft2Digital to make sure everything is formatted and rendered correctly.

Publish your book: Click Publish to publish your book on the selected platforms.

Similar to Amazon KDP, it usually takes a few hours for the book to be available on the selected platforms. Another important feature of Draft2Digital is the ability to publish the book on multiple sales platforms at the same time. Unlike KDP, which only publishes on Amazon, authors and publishers can publish their books on various platforms such as Apple Books, Barnes & Noble, Kobo, and many others. This opens up more opportunities for authors and publishers to reach their audience and increase their sales opportunities.

Another benefit of Draft2Digital is the wider range of publishing options. The platform offers a variety of tools and services that enable authors and publishers to better market and promote their books. This includes features like pre-orders, a way to share reading samples, and the ability to schedule discount promotions.

I, personally, find that Draft2Digital is a better option for authors and publishers than KDP. With D2D you can also deliver to KDP and thus manage all your publications from one account.

QR-CODE Draft2Digital

4. Affiliate Marketing

Recently, ChatGPT has proven to be a powerful tool for text generation and editing. It uses machine learning and natural language processing to create natural language text that is almost indistinguishable from human writing. This technology can also be used in affiliate marketing to generate mass blog articles and thereby increase monetization opportunities. In this article, we will discuss how ChatGPT can be used for this purpose.

Creation of blog articles

ChatGPT can be used to create blog articles related to a specific topic. You can simply feed ChatGPT a topic or keyword combination and then ask them to write an article about it. You can also set specific guidelines or writing styles to ensure the text meets your expectations.

Creation of product reviews

Affiliate marketing often refers to the promotion of products and services to earn commissions. ChatGPT allows you to create product reviews that detail how the product works and what its benefits are. You can also ask ChatGPT to create product comparisons to show how the advertised product compares to similar products.

Updating Content

One of the most difficult challenges when writing blog articles is making sure they stay fresh and relevant. With ChatGPT, you can update content quickly and easily by asking it to update the text accordingly or add new information.

Headline generation

Headlines are the most important part of any article, as they grab the reader's attention and entice them to read the article. With ChatGPT, you can generate headlines that are creative and engaging while summarizing the topic of the article.

Creation of social media posts

ChatGPT also allows you to create social media posts promoting your affiliate products. If you use this technology effectively, you can create masses of articles and thereby improve your chances of monetization in affiliate marketing.

Blogging and affiliate marketing is a way to make money by partnering with a company and promoting their products or services. When a reader of the blog buys a product or service through the affiliate link, the blogger earns a commission. Here are some steps you should follow to make money blogging and affiliate marketing:

1. Find affiliate partners: You can find affiliate programs from companies related to your blog topic, or sign up to affiliate networks to find different affiliate programs. You can also contact companies directly and request a partnership.

1. Write Informative Blog Articles: Write articles related to the products or services you want to promote. These articles should be helpful and informative to keep readers interested.

1. Place affiliate links in your articles: Place affiliate links in your articles to promote the products or services. These links should be well-placed and integrated into the article content to naturally draw attention to the product being promoted.

1. Promote your blog articles: Share your articles through social media, email newsletters, or other distribution channels to increase your readership. The more readers read your articles, the higher your chances of making money through affiliate links.

1. Analyze Results: Track how many clicks and sales are generated from your affiliate links. Use this data to understand which items and products are performing best and optimize your strategy accordingly.

1. Choose Appropriate Affiliate Programs: Select affiliate programs that offer good value for money and whose products or services are relevant to your readership.

1. Build an Engaged Readership: An engaged readership is key to the success of an affiliate marketing blog.

It is important to take a transparent and honest approach by communicating your affiliate partnerships clearly and focusing on products that offer added value for the readership.

4.1 Affiliate Marketing with ChatGPT and Search Engine Optimization

1. There are two main areas of search engine optimization:

On-Page Optimization and Off-Page Optimization.

On-page optimization refers to all optimization measures performed directly on the website itself. Here are some key aspects of on-page optimization:

- Keyword Research: Identify relevant keywords that potential visitors use to find your website.
- Content Optimization: Create high-quality, informative content that caters to user needs while paying attention to the keywords used.
- Structure of the website: A clear structure of your website makes navigation easier for users and search engine crawlers.
- Optimizing Meta Tags: Meta tags, such as title and meta description tags, help search engines better understand the content of your page.

Off-page optimization refers to all optimization measures performed outside the website to increase its relevance and authority. Here are some important aspects of off-page optimization:

1. Link Building: Building quality links from other websites to your website signals to search engines the relevance and authority of your website.

1. Social Media Marketing: Using social media can help increase awareness of your website and improve engagement with the target audience.

1. Brand Building: A strong brand can help users and search engines rank your website as more trustworthy and relevant.

These optimization measures are particularly important for blogs to increase visibility and reach, and thus generate more traffic and potential customers. By implementing on-page optimization and off-page optimization, bloggers can increase the organic reach of their content and thus increase the success of their affiliate marketing strategy.

4.2 Step-by-step guide to making money from an affiliate website

As mentioned, affiliate marketing is primarily about making money by creating websites and filling them with content that can then be found by users upon request in a search engine such as Google. To find a readership for the content created by ChatGPT, we have to find a niche again with this application as well.

The aim is therefore to create niche websites with as little effort as possible.

A niche website is a website that specializes in a specific niche or topic. It contains content geared towards a specific audience and can be related to anything from products and services to specific interests or hobbies.

The main purpose of a niche website is to target a specific audience and serve a specific need or interest. This can be done by creating informative articles, product reviews, tutorials, guides, and other content focused on the specific niche.

An example of a niche site might be one that focuses on home fitness equipment reviews. The website would then publish articles and reviews on various home fitness machines and equipment, targeting a target audience of people interested in exercising in their homes.

Niche websites can also be used for affiliate marketing. By recommending products or services relevant to the specific niche, niche website owners can earn a commission for each successful referral.

A niche website can be a great way to start a small online business, especially for people who have a passion or expertise in a particular niche and want to target an audience that shares similar interests.

At this point, it must be said obviously that you need to be familiar with web design or WordPress to create such niche sites. The content management system is easy to learn and if you want to work in affiliate marketing, a more in-depth understanding is a prerequisite. Let's kick it off!

1. For our case study, we created a page on the subject of "vegan dog food".
2. We also found this niche thanks to Mangools' KWFinder.
3. After the website structure has been created, the text content is created. ChatGPT becomes active for us.
4. So I'll use one of the top prompts that I introduced earlier.
5. Prompt: "I need an informative blog post on vegan dog food that will provide my readers with valuable and relevant information and convince them to compare my products."
6. The result: As pet owners, we know how important it is to provide our dogs with a balanced and healthy diet. Lately, interest in vegan dog food has increased as more pet owners look for sustainable and ethical options.

In this blog post, we will take a closer look at vegan dog food and discuss the pros and cons of this dietary option for our four-legged friends.

What is vegan dog food?

Vegan dog food is a nutritional option based on plant-based ingredients such as grains, vegetables, fruits, and legumes, and contains no animal-derived ingredients. There are many brands of vegan dog food on the market, all using different formulations and ingredients.

Benefits of vegan dog food

1. *Sustainability: A plant-based diet is more environmentally friendly than a meat-based diet because the production of meat is associated with high greenhouse gas emissions.*
2. *No Cruelty to Animals: The production of conventional dog food can involve cruelty to animals, including the cruel conditions of industrial animal husbandry. With vegan dog food, you avoid these practices.*
3. *Health: A vegan diet can also have health benefits for dogs. Some studies have indicated that a plant-based diet can reduce the risk of obesity, cancer, and other diseases.*

Disadvantages of vegan dog food

Lack of Nutrients: It is difficult to ensure that a vegan diet has all the nutrients dogs need. Dogs require certain amino acids found in meat products to stay healthy.

Digestive Issues: Some dogs may have trouble digesting plant-based proteins, which can lead to digestive issues.

Vet Control: A vegan diet requires careful monitoring by a veterinarian to ensure your dog is getting all the necessary nutrients.

Conclusion

The decision to feed your dog vegan or not is a personal choice. There are pros and cons to vegan dog food, and it is important to consider your dog's needs and plan their diet carefully. If you choose to follow a vegan diet, it's important to make sure your dog is getting all the nutrients they need to stay healthy. Monitoring by a veterinarian is recommended.

1. I think that's something to be proud of. If I still need more content, I would have the respective sub-items created again in more detail.
2. Something like this: Write an article about: "Sustainability: A plant-based diet is more environmentally friendly than a meat-based diet because the production of meat is associated with high greenhouse gas emissions."
3. The result: Recently, the topic of sustainability has become increasingly important as we have become more aware of how our way of life affects the environment and the resources of our planet. One of the easiest and most effective ways to reduce our ecological footprint is through what we eat. A plant-based diet is one of the most sustainable forms of nutrition out there.
4. The production of meat and animal products is associated with high emissions of greenhouse gases. Livestock farming is one of the largest sources of methane emissions, a potent greenhouse gas that is 25 times more potent than carbon dioxide. In addition, feeding animals is an inefficient process because animals need plenty of calories to grow and stay healthy. In fact, the production of meat and dairy requires about 10

times more resources than the production of plant-based foods.

A plant-based diet can therefore help to reduce the carbon footprint and fight climate change. Some studies have proved that a plant-based diet can reduce carbon emissions by up to 50% compared to a meat-based diet.

In addition, plants require less water and land to grow, which also contributes to sustainability. Unlike animal husbandry, which requires large amounts of water and land to raise and feed animals, crops can be grown in smaller areas and with less water.

A plant-based diet also has health benefits for individuals. A plant-based diet is typically high in fiber, vitamins, and minerals and low in saturated fat. Studies have indicated that a plant-based diet can reduce the risk of cardiovascular disease, diabetes, and cancer.

In summary, a plant-based diet is not only good for your health, but also environmentally friendly. By reducing meat consumption, we can reduce our carbon emissions, reduce water consumption and use our resources more effectively. Switching to a plant-based diet is an important step we can all take to promote sustainability and protect our environment.

1. *Google or search engines are not enthusiastic about AI-generated content. And so, it happens that the article in this pure form is very unlikely to be able to "tend". According to this, AI-generated content is not even indexed by search engines or rated as insufficient and accordingly users cannot find the content. However, we can easily work around this problem. With a rephrase tool like copy.ai's, another AI that rewrites the text in a way that Google considers it human-written.*

QR-Code copy.ai

1. The output is impressive. If you tinker around with the different content for a day, a website with about 30 subpages can be created quickly. A little search engine optimization and the niche site is ready. All this in 1-2 days. Not bad for a project that would have taken several weeks before AI tools like ChatGPT.

5. Freelancing with ChatGPT

The world of work has changed dramatically lately, particularly with the rise of online freelancer platforms. These platforms have enabled freelancers to search for work and offer their services all over the world without having to rely on traditional job markets. In this article, we will look at the benefits and challenges of working as a freelancer on platforms.

One benefit of working as a freelancer on platforms is flexibility. Freelancers can set their schedule and choose projects that match their skills and interests. Furthermore, there is often a wide variety of projects, allowing freelancers to broaden their skills and diversify their experiences.

Another challenge freelancers face on platforms is competition. Since platforms have many freelancers from all over the world, it can be difficult to stand out from the crowd and land jobs. Freelancers therefore need to focus on their skills and ensure their profiles and work samples are engaging and professional.

Another disadvantage of working as a freelancer on platforms is that it can be difficult to find a stable source of income. Since jobs on platforms are often project-based, there is no guarantee of ongoing work. It is therefore important as a freelancer to actively seek new opportunities on platforms and to build a solid relationship with existing clients.

An advantage of working as a freelancer on platforms is that there are often many jobs that allow freelancers to increase their earnings. On platforms, freelancers can often set their prices and apply for jobs that correspond to their price level. However, it is important to keep an eye on the market and prices to stay competitive.

As a freelancer, it is important to choose a job that you enjoy doing and that you want to stay with for the long term. If a customer chooses a freelancer, the placement is handled by the platform and a placement fee is due. The amount of this fee varies between 5% and 20% of the order value.

The advantages of freelancer platforms are manifold. On the one hand, as a freelancer, you have a greater reach and are found more easily by potential customers. On the other hand, you can use the platforms to expand your network and get new orders. Some platforms also offer additional services such as project management tools or payment processing to make the work process easier.

There are numerous freelancer platforms in German-speaking countries, including Freelancer.de, twago.de, upwork.com, fiverr.com, clickworker.com, projektwerk.com, 99designs.de, textbroker.de, machdudas.de and freelancermap.de. The decisive factors here are the size of the platform and the specialization. There are platforms that specialize in certain areas of activity such as design, writing or programming.

As a freelancer, it is important to compare the different platforms and choose the one that best suits your needs. In the appendix of the book you will find a list of the five most important platforms including the advantages and disadvantages in comparison.

In summary, freelancer platforms offer an excellent opportunity to find jobs and earn money as a freelancer. With a good presentation of your skills and a careful selection of platforms, you can be successful as a freelancer and receive long-term orders.

My personal top favorites, Fiverr and Upwork! I was able to generate strong sales on both platforms using AI.

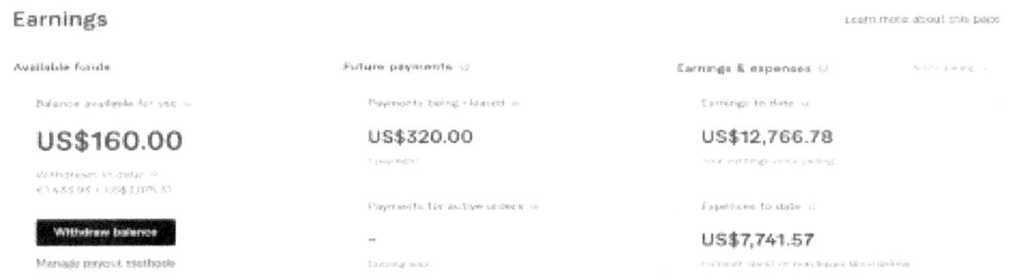

Quelle: Screenshot Earnings 2023 at Fiverr https://www.fiverr.com

5.1 How can you use AI to make money as a freelancer?

Creating copy texts as a freelancer. A copywriter, also known as a copywriter, is a professional copywriter who specializes in creating copywriting to promote products or services. Copywriting can be used in various fields, such as advertising, marketing or public relations.

A copywriter creates copy specifically designed to capture the attention of potential customers and persuade them to buy a product or use a service. This includes using persuasive words and phrases designed to get the reader to take a specific action, such as making a call, visiting a website, or buying a product.

A copywriter must be able to put themselves in the shoes of the target group and understand their needs, desires, and motivations. You must also be able to identify the unique features and benefits of a product or service and incorporate them into persuasive writing.

He must also be able to write clear and concise texts that will grab the reader's attention and make them engage with the product or service. At the same time, the text must be informative, relevant and provide the reader with all the necessary information to make an informed decision.

And in 2023, a good copywriter just needs to use the right prompts at ChatGPT. Here is the top selection.

1. "I'm looking for a [type of text] that directly addresses my [ideal customer persona]'s needs and issues and compels them to take [desired action] with a sense of urgency and a strong proposition.
2. "I need a [text type] that demonstrates the value and benefits of my [product/service] to [ideal customer personas] and convinces them to take [desired action] with social proof and credible elements."
3. "I'm looking for a [type of text] that clearly explains [ideal customer persona] the features and benefits of my [product/service] and convinces them to buy with a strong call-to-action."

4. "I need a [type of text] that gets my [ideal customer persona] feeling [emotions] about my [product/service] and persuades them to take a [desired action] with a sense of urgency."

5. "I'm looking for a [type of text] that builds trust and credibility with my [ideal customer persona] by highlighting the successes and testimonials of previous customers who have used my [product/service]."

6. "I need a [type of text] that clears my [ideal customer persona]'s objections and concerns about my [product/service] and convinces them to take [desired action]."

7. "I'm looking for a [text type] that introduces [ideal customer personas] to the unique features and benefits of my [product/service] and persuades them to buy."

8. "I need a [text type] that tells a story about my [product/service] and how it helped [the ideal customer persona] achieve their [goal] in a personable and compelling way."

9. "I'm looking for a [type of text] that will entice my [ideal customer persona] with a strong headline and hook, and then use compelling language and convincing evidence to convince them to take the [desired action]."

10. "I need a [type of text] that addresses the problems and needs of my [ideal customer persona] and shows them that my [product/service] is the solution they were looking for."

11. "I'm looking for a [type of text] that clearly and concisely explains to [the ideal customer persona] the features and benefits of my [product/service] and gets them to make a purchase."

1. "I need a [type of text] that gets my [ideal customer persona] to feel [emotions] about my [product/service] and convince them to take [desired action]."

2. "I'm looking for a [text type] that will convince [ideal customer persona] to enroll in my [program/subscription] by explaining the value and benefits they will receive."

3. "I need a [text type] that convinces [ideal customer persona] to buy my [product/service] by highlighting its unique benefits and addressing potential objections."

4. "Please write compelling [text] that speaks directly to my [ideal customer persona] and encourages them to take [desired action] on my [website/product]."

Cold email copywriter. A cold email copywriter is responsible for writing effective and engaging emails to reach potential customers or business partners who have not previously shown any interest in the products or services being offered.

Unlike warm emails, which are sent to people who already have some interest or relationship with the company, cold emails are unsolicited messages to people who may not be familiar with the company or brand.

A good cold email copywriter is able to write a compelling and personal email that will grab the recipient's attention and make them open, read, and ideally reply to the email or a to perform action.

This includes writing a clear subject line that motivates the recipient to open the email, as well as crafting a personalized message that addresses the recipient's needs and interests. A good cold email copywriter also understands the importance of a clear call-to-action that tells the recipient what they should do next.

The success of cold emails also depends on the quality of the address database used, as they are only successful if they are addressed to the right audience. A good cold email copywriter will therefore work closely with the marketing team to ensure emails are sent to the right people.

My top prompt choices for cold email

1. "I need a cold calling email idea that will engage my [ideal customer persona] with a unique and compelling perspective on [topic] and get them to take [desired action] on my [website/product] to perform."
2. "I'm looking for a cold calling email idea that will inspire trust and credibility with my [ideal customer persona] by underscoring my [company/brand's] expertise and professionalism."
3. "I need a cold calling email idea that will make a unique and compelling

offer to my [ideal customer persona] and compel them to take [desired action] with a sense of urgency and exclusivity."

4. "I'm looking for a cold email idea that shows my [ideal customer persona] the benefits and value of my [product/service] and convinces them to buy with a strong call-to-action. "

5. "I need a cold calling email idea that will engage my [ideal customer persona] with a personalized and targeted approach, and get them to take [desired action] with a clear and compelling message."

6. "I need a cold email idea that offers a behind-the-scenes look at my [company/brand] and convinces my [ideal customer persona] with a sense of authenticity and familiarity to [desired action] to do."

7. "I'm looking for a cold calling email idea that provides step-by-step instructions on how to use my [product/service] and my [ideal customer persona] with clear and compelling instructions on how to purchase emotional."

8. "I need a cold email idea that demonstrates how my [product/service] can solve the specific problems and needs of my [ideal customer persona] in a personable and engaging way."

9. "I'm looking for a cold calling email idea that will showcase my [product/service] unique selling points and get my [ideal customer persona] to buy with a sense of urgency and exclusive offers."

10. "I need a cold calling email idea that will compare my [product/service] to similar offerings on the market and convince my [ideal customer persona] to choose us with clear and compelling evidence ."

11. "I'm looking for a cold calling email idea that will attract my [ideal customer persona] with a personable and authentic message, and then convince them with a strong call-to-action and compelling visuals that will [desired action] to perform."

12. "I need a cold calling email idea that will provide my [ideal customer persona] with valuable and relevant information about [topic] and get them to take [desired action] with a clear and compelling message."

13. "I'm looking for a cold calling email idea that will resolve my [ideal customer persona]'s objections and concerns about my [product/service] and persuade them with a sense of urgency to take [desired action]. seize."

14. "I need a cold calling email idea that will establish credibility and authority with my [ideal customer persona] by showcasing the success stories of previous customers who have used my [product/service]."

Write YouTube or video scripts:

A video script writer writes the screenplay for a video. The script serves as a guide for producing a video and includes descriptions of the plot, characters, dialogue and visual elements. A videoscript writer works closely with the director or producer to ensure the script meets the needs of the project. The video script writer's job is to ensure that the script is interesting and engaging, that it conveys the video's message, and that it resonates with viewers. A video script writer must be creative and imaginative, able to present complex information in a clear and concise manner.

My top prompt choices:

1. "I need a YouTube ad script that showcases my [product/service] unique selling points and persuades my [ideal customer persona] to make a purchase with a sense of urgency and exclusive offers.

2. "I'm looking for a YouTube ad script that will attract my [ideal customer persona] with a personable and authentic message, then compel them to take [desired action] with a strong call-to-action and compelling visuals."

3. "I'm looking for a YouTube ad script that will build trust and credibility with my [ideal customer persona] by highlighting the successes and testimonials of previous customers who have used my [product/service]."

4. "I need a YouTube ad script that educates my [ideal customer persona] about a specific [topic] and gets them to take [desired action] on my [website/product]."

5. "I'm looking for a YouTube ad script that addresses my [ideal customer persona's] needs and issues head-on, compelling them to take [desired action] with a sense of urgency and a strong offer."

6. "I need a YouTube ad script that will provide my [ideal customer persona] with valuable and relevant information and get them to take

[desired action] on my [website/product]."

7. "I'm looking for a YouTube ad script that will engage my [ideal customer persona] with a unique and compelling perspective on [topic] and compel them to take [desired action] on my [website/product]."

8. "I need a YouTube ad script that will address the issues and needs of my [ideal customer persona] and show them that my [product/service] is the solution they were looking for."

9. "I'm looking for a YouTube ad script that clearly explains the features and benefits of my [product/service] to my [ideal customer persona] and convinces them to buy with a sense of urgency."

10. "I need a YouTube ad script that tells a story about my [product/service] and how it helped the [ideal customer persona] achieve their [goal] in a personable and engaging way."

11. "I'm looking for a YouTube ad script that demonstrates the value and benefits of my [product/service] to my [ideal customer persona] and gets them to take [desired action] with a strong offer and a clear call to action. "

12. "I need a YouTube ad script that will resolve my [ideal customer persona]'s objections and concerns about my [product/service] and convince them with a sense of urgency to take [desired action]."

13. "I'm looking for a YouTube ad script that will entice my [ideal client persona] with a strong headline and hook, and then convince them to take [desired action] with compelling language and compelling evidence."

14 "I need a YouTube ad script that introduces my [ideal customer persona] to the unique features and benefits of my [product/service] and convinces them to buy with social proof and credible elements."

1. "I'm looking for a YouTube ad script that will introduce my [product/service] to my [ideal client].

Freelancing as a virtual assistant. A Virtual Assistant (VA) is a self-employed person who performs administrative, organizational and/or technical tasks for clients remotely. The work of a virtual assistant can be very different depending on the needs and can extend to different areas.

The tasks of a virtual assistant usually include:

Scheduling and coordination of appointments

E-mail communication and management

Preparation of reports, presentations and other documents

Database management and data entry

research and compilation of information

Accounting and Invoicing

Social media management and content creation

Customer Service and Support

Organization of trips and events

A virtual assistant can offer its services to both individuals and companies. Working remotely allows her to support clients in different countries and time zones while demonstrating her flexibility and adaptability.

The work of a virtual assistant requires high organizational ability, good communication skills and technical knowledge in different fields to be able to complete the different tasks effectively and efficiently. Or just a ChatGPT access with the right prompts.

A virtual assistant can use ChatGPT in different ways to improve their work and make it more efficient. Here are some examples:

1. Research Assistance: ChatGPT can assist in researching information needed for virtual assistant work. The model can answer questions and link to relevant resources to find information faster and more accurately.

1. Task Automation: ChatGPT can also be used to automate repetitive

tasks, like answering frequently asked questions or creating default answers. By using pre-programmed responses and scripts, the virtual assistant can save time and focus on more complex tasks.

2. Content Creation: ChatGPT can also be used to create content, such as blog posts, social media posts, and emails. The virtual assistant can hire ChatGPT to create a draft, which they can then revise and customize.

1. Improving Customer Service: ChatGPT can also be used to improve customer service. The virtual assistant can use ChatGPT to quickly and accurately answer questions from customers or to solve problems. This can help increase customer satisfaction and positively position the company.

6.ChatGPT while programming

In today's world of technology, programming has become an important part of our daily lives. Many of us use apps, programs and websites created by developers on a daily basis to make our life easier and more efficient. But programming can also be challenging, especially for beginners who are new to the syntax and logic of programming languages.

This is where ChatGPT comes in. As an advanced language model based on GPT-3.5 architecture, ChatGPT has the potential to help developers around the world to code. With extensive knowledge of various programming languages and technologies, ChatGPT can act as a virtual assistant and provide valuable assistance in solving problems, optimizing code and developing new applications. In this book, I will detail how ChatGPT can support developers in their daily workflow and how to get the most out of this innovative tool.

ChatGPT is an advanced language model based on the GPT 3.5 architecture. It can help developers around the world with programming by providing valuable assistance in solving problems, optimizing code and developing new applications. In this article, I will give you a step-by-step guide on how to use ChatGPT while coding.

Step 1: Set up ChatGPT. To use ChatGPT you need an API key. Go to the website of the provider you want to use and follow the instructions to set up an account. After registration you will receive an API key which you will need to access ChatGPT.

Step 2: Configure the developer environment. To use ChatGPT, you need to configure your developer environment. You can use an integrated development environment (IDE) like Visual Studio Code or a text editor app like Sublime Text to do this. Make sure your environment includes the required dependencies and libraries to communicate with the ChatGPT API.

Step 3: Create a connection to the ChatGPT API. To connect to the ChatGPT API, you need to integrate the API key you received in the first step into your developer environment. To achieve this, you can use a library like "requests" to make HTTP requests to the API and process the results.

Step 4: Using ChatGPT while coding. After connecting to the ChatGPT API, you can use ChatGPT while coding. Let's say you want to write a function that calculates the square of a number. You could write this function like this:

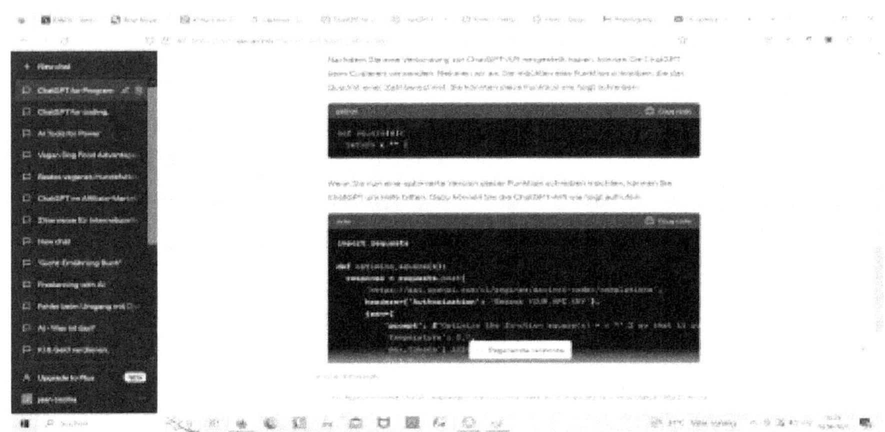

Now, if you want to write an optimized version of this function, you can ask ChatGPT for help. To complete this, you can call the ChatGPT API as follows:

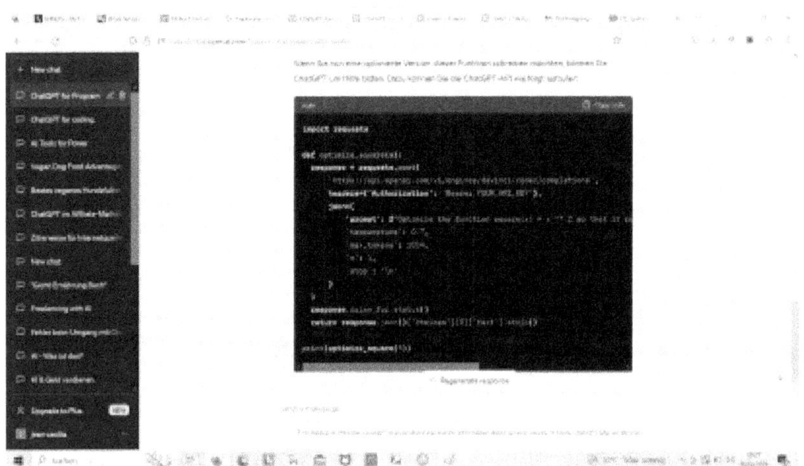

This code calls the ChatGPT API to generate an optimized version of the "square" function. The API is called with a text prompt that describes the desired optimization. The API then returns a response containing the optimized code. The optimized code is then output.

With its powerful features and capabilities, ChatGPT offers a variety of benefits that can improve coding efficiency and accuracy.

Improved coding efficiency and speed. ChatGPT can help developers speed up and improve the coding process. It can quickly and easily generate code suggestions based on developer's needs. This can accelerate code development by allowing developers to write code in real time without worrying about how to write each line. Using ChatGPT also allows developers to react more quickly to issues and optimize code to improve performance.

Avoid errors by checking code with ChatGPT. One of ChatGPT's most important features is the ability to review code and find bugs. ChatGPT can check the syntax of code to ensure it is spelled correctly. It can also identify faulty or inefficient blocks of code and suggest a better solution to the developer. Using ChatGPT in error prevention can help the applications built on the code to be more reliable and stable.

Deeper understanding of code through ChatGPT suggestions. ChatGPT can also help developers get a better understanding of the code by suggesting improvements. If developers are having trouble writing code, ChatGPT can offer suggestions on how to optimize the code. This can help developers learn more about the code and better understand how it works. By using ChatGPT, developers can also learn to make better code decisions by learning from the model's suggestions.

However, despite its advantages, there are also challenges to using ChatGPT when coding.

Limited ability of ChatGPT in solving complex problems. ChatGPT is a language model trained on human speech. Although it is capable of generating simple code suggestions and finding bugs, it has limited abilities in solving complex problems. It may have difficulty understanding and generating complex code structures and architectures required by some applications. In such cases, it may be necessary to bring in additional expertise and experience from experienced developers to handle the complexity of the issues.

Difficulty checking security of code through ChatGPT. Another problem with using ChatGPT when coding is the difficulty of verifying the security of the code. ChatGPT can generate code suggestions and find bugs, but it is unable to detect or fix security issues. It may even come up with suggestions for insecure code that is vulnerable to attack. It is therefore important that developers manually check the security of the code they write and ensure that it is free of security vulnerabilities.

ChatGPT is a useful tool that can help developers code by generating code suggestions and finding bugs. However, there are also challenges in using ChatGPT in coding, especially in solving complex problems and verifying the security of the code. Developers should be aware of these challenges and be able to address them to ensure their applications are secure, reliable, and efficient.

Index

Here is a summary of all the basic and used AI tools

https://chat.openai.com/ > ChatGPT

https://pictory.ai > Image and Video Creation Discount Code: jean91

https://www.copy.ai > Paraphrasing and Copywriting

https://mangools.com/> Keyword Tool

https://www.draft2digital.com/book-publishing > Worldwide Publishing

One more thing,

I'm excited to share my book with you and hope it provides you with valuable insight and information. As you browse the pages, you will in some places come across links contained within the text.

I want to be transparent about these links and explain how they work. Affiliate links are a way for me to earn a small commission for the products or services I recommend. This is done at no additional cost to you and helps support the creation and maintenance of this book.

If you are interested in one of the tools presented, I would be happy if you use the partner link that I provide in the text. Not only do you get a great product or service, you also support the work that went into creating this book.

Kindly note that I only include links for products or services that I, personally, use and believe in. I strive to give you honest and helpful recommendations.

Thank you for considering my affiliate links, and I hope you have found my book a valuable resource.

Best regards

John Du Jardin